Lake
COMO

Edizioni KINA Italia/Eurografica

Index

Lake Como

Deeply eroded valleys, massive moraine deposits, erratic boulders carried by glaciers and torrential waters that feed one of the deepest lakes in Europe: this is the legacy left by the ice of the Quaternary era in the Como area. 12,000 years after the last Ice Age, the climate is very different from what it was then – in fact it is famed for its mildness. Chestnut and conifer woods and large stretches of pasture land now cover the mountain slopes. Exotic species grow alongside the cypresses and bay trees typical of the Mediterranean maquis while flourishing citrus trees, palm trees, azaleas, cacti and camellias have made the gardens of the ancient patrician villas famous. Lake Como (also known as Lario), surrounded by imposing mountains like the Grigne range and Mount Legnone (2609 m), stretches for 50 km between Como and Sorico, reaching its maximum width of

4.4 km between Fiumelatte and Cadenabbia. The lake is mainly fed by the River Adda, which joins it at Colico, and splits into the Como and Lecco branches at Bellagio, but it receives waters from numerous streams around its entire perimeter. Just one small island, Isola Comacina, emerges from the depths of the lake, while at one point, between Nesso and Argegno, the lake bed plunges to 410 metres: the greatest depth of any European lake. The transverse valleys excavated by the glaciers generate a complex wind system, once exploited for commercial navigation. Nowadays, the two dominant breezes and a myriad of sudden unstable winds are the delight and despair of the many yachtsmen on the lake. The first human settlements in the area date back to 4500 B.C., but it was not until 3500 years later that the area developed a true civilisation as a result

of contact with a variety of populations, such as the Ligurians, the Insubrian Celts and the Etruscans. The oppidum was not formed until around the 6th or 5th century B.C., and to judge by the Cà Morta necropolis in the Spina Verde Park, east of Como, it must have been a large settlement. The region then fell to the Insubrians, who only left in 196 B.C., when they were driven out by the Romans. After a period of decline, the area rapidly recovered, and attracted numerous colonists. Thanks to the development of the road network and water communications, reclamation and fortification works, by 59 B.C. the oppidum was a major trade, culture and tourism centre called Novum Comum. Christian penetration began in the 3rd century A.D., inaugurating the power of the bishops, which was to remain strong for centuries. The Lombard conquest, invasion by the Franks and raids by the Hungarians did not affect what was by now a well-established cultural identity. This difficult period is recalled by the tower of Castel Baradello, in the Spina Verde park. This is all that remains of the ancient fortifications, which probably dated from prehistoric times, and had a defensive function in the Roman and

Byzantine eras and throughout the Middle Ages. In the 12th century the area became a target of the expansionist aims of Milan. In 1100 Como struck up an alliance with Federico Barbarossa, but eventually had to surrender to domination by the Viscontis, becoming an integral part of the Milanese territory, with which it was to remain linked forever. The flourishing manufacturing and mining activities of the Renaissance era were followed by a slow decline under Spanish domination. Things were made worse by the harsh measures taken by Carlo Borromeo against the Protestant reforms of Calvinist Switzerland, but the worst was to come in 1630, when the area was devastated by plague, brought by the Landsknechts. In the early 18th century, unexpected salvation came in the form of sericulture and the silk industry, which was to make the Como area world-famous, partly thanks to the administration of Maria Teresa of Austria. At the same time, the metallurgical industry developed in the Lecco area, and figures like Giuseppe Parini and Alessandro Volta emerged in the literary and scientific fields. In 1796, Napoleon's troops defeated the Austrian army and marched into Como. Three years later,

Lombardy was incorporated in the Cisalpine Republic. This led to a crisis in the Como area. Its main industries no longer had an outlet on the German market, and taxes designed to finance the Napoleonic campaigns bled dry the local authorities. After the Congress of Vienna in 1815, Lombardy returned under Austrian rule, but the civil service had changed, and the economic crisis was very serious. A recovery took place in the second half of the 19th century. The introduction of spinning machines and mechanical looms contributed to the growth of industry and a major urban drift. Similar progress was made in the metallurgical industry, and rail and lake transport infrastructures grew at the same time. By the start of the 20th century industry was well established, but social tensions and workers' demands also arose. Spared by the First World War, the Como area experienced the Fascist period with a kind of indifference, despite the miners' and millers' revolt in Introbio and Cortabio, the closure of some newspapers, and a few episodes of violence

Villa Carlotta gardens

Villa Olmo

by organised Fascist gangs. As elsewhere, the local authorities renewed structures and carried out major development work.

The political atmosphere was very different in the Second World War: small partisan formations were already active by 1943, their ranks increased by young men who refused compulsory recruitment by the Social Republic. It was in this area that the Fascist period came to an end, with the capture of Mussolini near Dongo. The post-war years brought a strong economic recovery, which was to give the region the highest per capita income in Italy. Although foreign competition has now reduced the importance of Como's silk mills on world markets, Como still maintains its tradition of high quality, especially in the field of design. In addition to traditional crafts, the major contribution to the local economy is made by advanced services and tourism. In addition, the foundation of Insubria University in 1988 rendered the area independent of Milan for university teaching.

Varenna, Villa Monastero

Como

Nestling between the lake and the mountains, Como is a frontier town in geographical terms, forming a natural bridge between the Po Valley and the countries beyond the Alps. In practice, it acts as a funnel for people and goods to meet and pass through. In terms of tourism, it provides a good starting point for short excursions: various boat trips are offered from Piazza Cavour, on the lakeside, returning by evening. Even those who don't venture outside the town will find plenty to see, such as the traditional Baradello festival, while art lovers can view a host of art treasures.

Within the ancient walls

The area within the Mediaeval walls, which has long been a pedestrian precinct, offers visitors a kind of journey back in time: its layout reflects the route of the ancient Roman roads, and many houses are pre-17th century. The walls, which have mostly disappeared, surround a quadrilateral between Via Nazario Sauro, Viale Cesare Battisti, Via Varese, Via Cavallotti and the lakeside promenade, with Piazza Cavour and its 19th-century palazzi. The centre of this older area is the cathedral of Santa Maria Maggiore and the adjacent Broletto, a 13th-century building made of grey, white and red marble, practically built onto the contemporary Town Hall Tower. The cathedral has an attractive Gothic façade dating from the late 15th century, embellished by three portals, sculptures by Giovanni Rodari and sons, and a rose window by Luchino Scarabota. Its construction was commenced in 1396 by Lorenzo degli Spazzi, and only finished in 1740, when the cupola by Filippo Juvara was added. The cathedral houses works by Bernardino Luini, Tommaso Rodari and Gaudenzio Ferrari. The wooden altar dedicated to Sant'Abbondio is by Angelo del Maino, while the high altar, made of marble, onyx and gilded bronze, is the work of 17th-century artists, as are the two large organs. The two 9th-century lions that support the fonts come from the ancient church of Santa Maria Maggiore, which was dismantled to make room for the cathedral. Oddly, the statues on the two plinths next to the main door represent two non-Christian personalities, Pliny the Elder and Pliny the Younger, who spent a great deal of time in the area. Behind the cathedral, just outside the walls, is the former Fascist Party Headquarters, one of the major architectural works of the Fascist era. Built in 1932

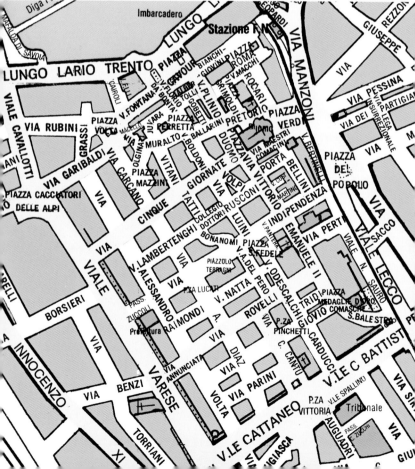

with the strictness typical of that style, it was designed by architect Giuseppe Terragni, and is now the headquarters of the Italian Finance Police. Near the cathedral, in piazza Grimaldi, stands the Church of San Giacomo. It once had six spans more than the present building, and apparently also had twin belltowers, but it was partly demolished to make way for the cathedral. The

The former Fascist Party Headquarters, G. Terragni

nearby Bishop's Palace, dating from the year 1000, which has also undergone numerous alterations, still retains some 17th-century tapestries and the ancient chapel of S. Michele, which stands on the site of an existing early Christian building. The small palazzo of Cardinal Branda Castiglioni, with its elegant 15th-century loggia, the Romanesque church of San Provino, and Palazzo Rodari Odescalchi, which houses the town's library, give onto Piazza Roma. Palazzo Pedraglio and Palazzo Pantera, both dating from the Renaissance era, stand opposite one another in Via Rodari. On arriving in Via Rusconi we see Palazzo

San Giacomo

Rusca, a 16th-century residence which was altered on various occasions in the 1960s. Next, we continue along Via Vittorio Emanuele, skirting Palazzo Porta Cernezzi, which houses the Town Hall, and come out in Piazza San Fedele, once the city marketplace. There stands the church of San Fedele, its interior embellished with Renaissance and Baroque paintings and frescoes, and Romanesque decorations. The 5th-century fonts were rescued from the early Christian church of Sant'Eufemia, which was demolished to make way for San Fedele. Not far away are the Paolo Giovio Civic Archaeological Museum, the Giuseppe Garibaldi Risorgimento Museum and the Civic Art Collections, housed in an attractive 17th-century building in the Porta Torre direction. After passing through Porta Torre (Tower Gate), which has surveyed the road to Milan since 1100, we find ourselves in Piazza Vittoria, with the statue of Giuseppe Garibaldi.

Palazzo Pedraglio

Palazzo Pantera

Bishop's Palace

Palazzo Rusca

Palazzo Commerciale Italiana

San Fedele – façade

Palazzo Cernezzi (Town Hall)

San Fedele – apse

Piazza San Fedele

Paolo Glovio Civic Museum

Porta Torre (Tower Gate)

Garibaldi Museum

Outside the walls

Beyond Porta Torre we can follow a route that visits several historic monuments, and then return to the lakeside promenade. The first stop is the Cittadella della Seta (Silk Citadel), which houses the museum that illustrates the history of Como through the industrial revolution. Founded in 1990 in the premises of the Silk Institute to house material collected since the Eighties, it shows all the stages that lead from the silkworm to the finished product. From here, we continue along Via Ambrosoli, Via Giulio Cesare and Via Roosevelt to the basilica consecrated to Sant'Abbondio, fourth bishop of Como and patron saint of the town, built in 1000 on the site of an existing 4th-century church. It was altered several times by the Benedictine monks over the years, and was partly restored to its original state in the 19th century. The interior of the austere basilica has a nave and four aisles lined with columns, a wooden ceiling, and frescoes by an anonymous 14th-century Lombard master

Fountain in Piazza Camerlata   *View from Castel Baradello*

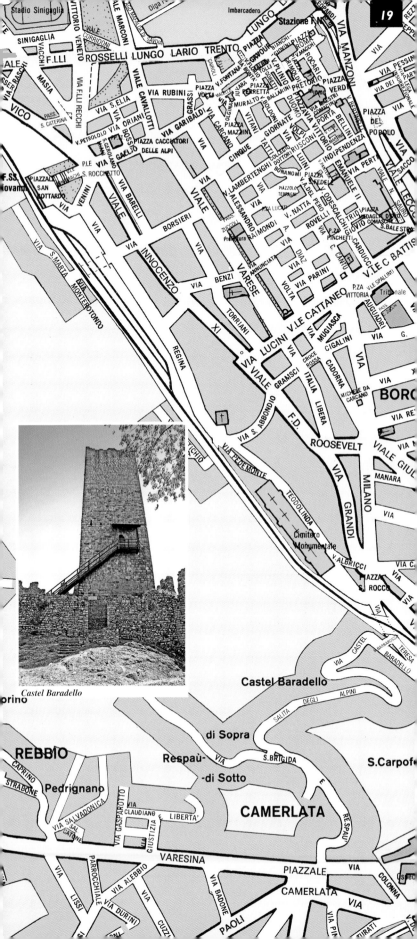

Castel Baradello

discovered during the latest restoration work. The nearby sanctuary of the Crucifix or church of the Annunziata, with an attractive façade by Luigi Fontana, contains frescoes by Innocenzo Carloni. Along the route we pass the former Tintoria Apparecchiatura e Stamperia Comense (Como Dying and Printing Works), then Ticosa, once the main factory of the town, but now in ruins. By following Via Regina Teodolinda, which runs alongside the Spina Verde Regional Park, we return to the town centre and continue along the lakeside promenade.

Piazza Vittoria

San Bartolomeo

San Carpoforo

Church of Sant'Orsola

Sant'Abbondio – interior

Sant'Abbondio

Church of the Crucifix

Walls of the Old Town

Viale Varese

The lakeside promenade

From Piazza Cavour, looking towards the lake, we find ourselves in front of a semicircle from which two routes can be chosen: Villa Geno to the right, and Villa Olmo to the left. If we choose the Villa Olmo route, we will come almost immediately to the Antonio Ratti Foundation's Textile Museum, then the European Resistance monument, and not far away the Volta Mausoleum, which was erected in 1927 to commemorate the first centenary of the death of inventor Alessandro Volta, and houses the instruments he used for his studies. Next we come to the "rationalist quarter", another work by Terragni dating from the early 20th century. A good example of the style of the period is the flamboyant

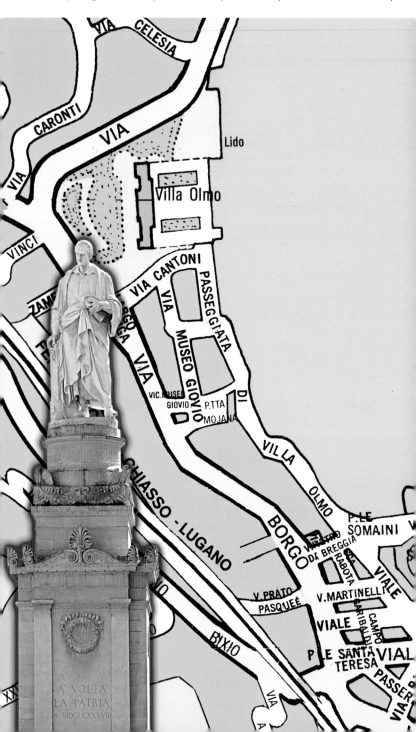

Novum Comun, a block of flats that the locals humorously refer to as "the Ocean Liner". Continuing to the left we come to the ancient Borgo Vico, once separate from the rest of the town. This section of the lakeside walk was reopened in 1957 to connect the lovely 18th-century villas overlooking the lake: Villa Scacchi, Villa Gallia, Villa Parravicini, Villa Mandolfo and Villa Saporiti, also known as "the Rotunda", which houses the Provincial Council's offices. Here stands the church of San Giorgio, built in the late 17th century on the ruins of a church dating from the year 1000. Behind the Baroque façade by Agostino Silva, the interior houses some exquisite frescoes by Gian Paolo Recchi.

Piazza Cavour

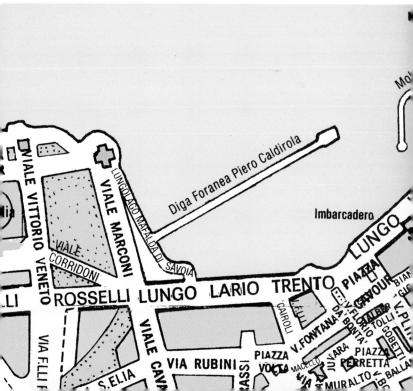

Piazza Cavour

Piazza Alessandro Volta

Volta Temple

War Memorial

Villa Pallavicino

Villa Saporiti

...atti Foundation

European Resistance Monument

Como Flying Club

Palazzo Resta Pallavicini, known as "The Rotunda"

...illa Patrizia

Villa Olmo

If we choose the route to the right which leads to Villa Geno, we first come to Piazza Matteotti, and the old Ferrovie Nord railway station with its glass and sheet metal roof. We then enter the Borgo Sant'Agostino district, said to be so old that it dates from the time of Novum Comum. Nearly all the houses in this district, which was originally the dockers' quarter, have been renovated, but not the church of Sant'Agostino, which still retains 17th-century frescoes, paintings and stuccoes behind a façade erected in the 14th century by the Augustinian monks of San Tommaso. The building underwent some alterations towards the end of the 18th century, but the origi-nal structure was later restored. Finally we come to Villa Geno, designed by Giacomo Tazzini for the Cornaggia-Medici family in the mid-19th century. Now owned by the town council, it has a jetty, park and restaurant open to the public, and serves as a conference and exhibition centre. Just before reaching the Villa we see one of the structures best-loved by the residents of Como: the funicular railway, which takes passengers 500 metres up to Brunate in just a few minutes. Inaugurated in 1894 it has now been electrified, but was steam-driven for 40 years. The old "machine room" can be visited in the station at the top.

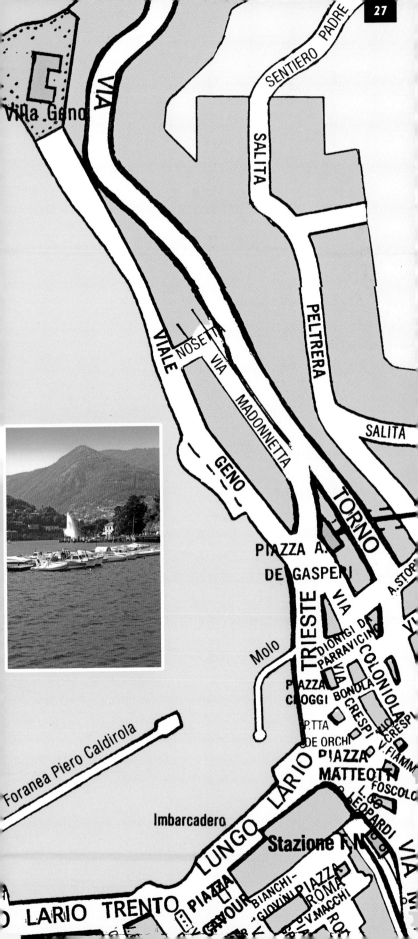

Villa Geno

VIA

SENTIERO PADRE

SALITA

PELTRERA

SALITA

VIALE

NOSETTA

VIA

MADONNETTA

GENO

TORNO

PIAZZA A.
DE GASPERI

A. STOR

VIA
TRIESTE

DIONIGI DE
PARRAVICINO

VIA

COLONIOLA

PIAZZA
C. LOGGI

BONOLA

CRESPI

V. CRESPI

P.TTA
DE ORCHI

V. FIAMM

Molo

PIAZZA
MATTEOTTI

FOSCOLO

L. GO
LEOPARDI

VIA

Foranea Piero Caldirola

LUNGO

LARIO

Imbarcadero

Stazione F.M.

PIAZZA
CAVOUR

BIANCHI-
GIOVINI

PIAZZA
ROMA

V. MACCHI

LARIO TRENTO

Piazza De Gasperi

Church of S. Agostino

Ferrovie Nord railway station

Villa Geno

Lungolago Trieste

Funicular station

Brunate

Nestling on the hillside 500 metres above sea level, Brunate has a privileged position overlooking the town of Como and the lake. Archaeological finds date the first settlement at the 5th century B.C.. In the Middle Ages, Como was an independent comune for a time, but it was inevitably subjugated by Como, which restricted its independence. Its elevated position, once of great strategic importance, has made it a popular resort for over 200 years, and although its fame has declined somewhat since the 19th century, the beauty of its Art Nouveau villas and their magnificent gardens has never faded. The church of Sant'Andrea, renovated in the 19th century, is worth a visit; it is decorated with 18th-century frescoes by Gian Paolo Recchi and contains relics of a much venerated nun, the Blessed Maddalena Alberici. A spectacular view can be seen from the top of the Faro Voltiano

(Volta Lighthouse), built in 1927 for the centenary of the death of Alessandro Volta. This is the most attractive viewpoint, but there are many others in the vicinity: Piazzale Bonacossa, the rotundas of Via Monterosa and Parco Marenghi, the Belvedere of via Pirotta, and finally the Pissarottino, where a spring renowned for its waters gushes forth. Brunate is also a starting point for numerous excursions into the mountains. The best-known is the "Backbone of the Lario Triangle" which connects Brunate to Bellagio; other interesting destinations are Via delle Colme, which starts from the exit of the funicular railway and leads to Mount Bollettone, and the route to Mount Piatto, where the numerous erratic boulders are of geological interest.

Volta lighthouse

Garzola Superiore

Villa Olmo

Villa Olmo (Elm Villa) is named after a gigantic elm tree which, according to legend, dated from the time of Pliny the Elder. The elm no longer survives, but the magnificent park surrounding the villa is still a classic example of an Italianate garden. Built in 1782 by Simone Cantoni for Marquis Odescalchi, it had various owners until 1925, when it became the property of the Town Council. Since then it has been used as a cultural centre for various activities, including those of the Alessandro

Volta Scientific Culture Centre. The villa, with its neoclassical façade, has very elegant interiors: the Mirror Room, the Oval (or Nuptial) Room, the Bacchus Room, the Ballroom, the Olympus Room, with frescoes by Domenico Pozzi, and the Music Room, with a wealth of decorations, including a large painting on the ceiling attributed to the Pozzi brothers. Also famous are the Odescalchi chapel and the little theatre, a masterpiece of acoustics with frescoes by Ernesto Fontana.

Cernobbio

Cernobbio, located close to Como and to the Swiss border, has a historic centre with some 16th-century houses. Nestling on the slopes of Mount Bisbino, on the western side it opens onto the lake, with its Art Nouveau jetty standing in the middle of a public park. Situated on the ancient Via Regina, its original name, Coenobium, derives from a Cluniac monastery that stood in the Villa Erba area. It includes some hamlets with panoramic views such as Piazza Santo Stefano, Casnedo and Rovenna, and various textile factories once operated in the area.

The trout-filled River Breggia which runs through the town was famous for its water mills. Cernobbio is an élite resort; it hosts exhibitions, congresses and international encounters at various levels, which find a worthy setting in the peace of the lake and the prestigious architecture of the villas where they are held. The best-known is Villa d'Este and Villa Erba, built in the early 20th century by the Erba family, owners of one of the major Italian pharmaceutical companies. It was the home of film director Luchino Visconti,

son of Carla Erba and Giuseppe Visconti di Modrone, who died there in 1976, and is now owned by the town council. Another conference venue is Villa Bernasconi, a magnificent example of the Art Nouveau style. Davide Bernasconi, founder of a textile company which was one of the driving forces of the local economy for many years, commissioned the design from architect Alfredo Campanini in the early 20th century. No less interesting are the 16th-century Villa Pizzo, Villa Besana (18th century), Villa Fontanelle, which belonged to fashion designer Gianni Versace, and the neo-classical Villa Fasana. Churches worth a visit include the parish church of San Vincenzo, which has been much renovated but still retains the original nucleus dating from 1100, Santa Maria delle Grazie and San Michele in the hamlet of Rovenna.

Villa d'Este

The first nucleus of the villa dates from the second half of the 16th century, when architect Pellegrino Tibaldi designed a structure consisting of two separate buildings joined by a portico for Cardinal Tolomeo Gallio. In time the original design was modified, and in the 18th century it became a three-storey building with a central section and two side wings. The history of the villa reflects that of its inhabitants, which reads like something out of a novel. After 200 years the ownership of the villa passed to Marquis Calderara, whose wife had an affair with Napoleonic General Domenico Pino; Pino killed the Marquis in a duel, married his widow and became the owner of the villa. On the fall of Napoleon the villa passed to Caroline of

Brunswick, Princess of Wales, who changed its original name, Villa del Garrovo, to the present name, and entertained lavishly there. When the princess returned to England the villa was abandoned until it was bought by Baron Ciani, and in 1873, after further alterations, it was turned into a hotel. Over the years, the Napoleon room (so called because the Emperor's initial is woven into the tapestry) has remained intact, and the Italianate garden, with its attractive nymph fountain and cypress avenue, is still very similar to the original. Some period decorations still survive, together with paintings and sculptures like the statues of Adam and Eve by Della Porta, and Cupid and Venus, carved in Canova's bottega.

Moltrasio

Moltrasio, which is formed by a number of hamlets situated on the slopes of Mount Bisbino, was once famous for the grey stone quarried in the mountains, and was already a well-known resort in the 19th century, as demonstrated by the numerous villas, which had many famous guests. Sicilian composer Vincenzo Bellini (1801-35), to whom the monument in Via Regina Vecchia is dedicated, spent a great deal of time at Villa Erker Hocevar, where he composed La Sonnambula, and Villa Passalacqua, where he composed La Straniera. The 18th-century Villa Passalacqua has a huge Italianate garden with terraces sloping down to the lake, and the interior is decorated with some excellent frescoes by Andrea Appiani. Villa Fasola (or Villa delle Magnolie) and Villa Ghisio are particularly interesting. Churches worth a visit include the 15th-century parish church of S. Martino in the hamlet of Borgo, with paintings by Gian Paolo Recchi and a polyptych by Alvise de Donati, and the church of S. Agata in the hamlet of Crotti, with its typical bare stone structure and external frescoes depicting scenes from the martyrdom of St. Agatha.

Argegno

This village, with just over 600 inhabitants, is situated on the Regina road, at the start of Val d'Intelvi. Founded by a Roman consul, it stands in the middle of an inlet of the lake in a particularly protected position, and the Telo river, overlooked by the mediaeval centre, flows through it. The river once drove watermills, and an old stone bridge still joins the two banks, where the old Via Regina used to run. In the characteristic streets, there is still a smithy dating from the second half of the 18th century, with its characteristic hammer. In view of its strategic position, Argegno was part of an extensive system of defences that included a 13th-century castle, only the bottom part of which still survives. Interesting churches include the fairly recent Chiesa della

Trinità and the 18th-century church of S. Anna, where some of the original frescoes, decorations and carved furniture still survive. The town is the ideal starting point for motoring or walking tours of Val d'Intelvi. A cable car takes passengers quickly up to Pigra, at an altitude of over 800 m, where the small church of S. Margherita offers a magnificent view over the lake. Lanzo d'Intelvi, Valsolda and Lake Lugano can easily be reached by car.

Isola Comacina

Isola Comacina, opposite Ossuccio and Sala Comacina in the gulf between Argegno and the Làvedo peninsula, is the only island in Lake Como. It is not far from the west shore, and resembles a large cliff entirely covered in trees. The part of the lake that separates it from the shore is called Zoca de l'Oli (basin of oil), because its waters are always as smooth as the oil still made in some parts of the area. The ancient history of the island is demonstrated by the remains of homes dating from Roman times, late Mediaeval fortifications and early Christian churches. In the 5th century Abbondio, Bishop of Como, built the basilica of S. Eufemia, the foundations of which were rediscovered in 1914. The island was besieged several times during the Longobard domination. The best-known siege was suffered by Byzantine governor Francione, who took refuge on the island with a large treasure and had to

surrender to King Autari, husband of Queen Theodolinda. Later, the island often provided refuge for rebels and escaping authorities. In general, ecclesiastical influence increased over the centuries, and some antagonism towards Como developed. During the 10-year war between Como and Milan, the island supported Milan against Federico Barbarossa, and fierce repression by the Como army led to its total destruction in 1169. Thereafter the island lost its importance, and it was wholly abandoned until Augusto Caprani managed to buy it in the early 20th century. It was bequeathed to King Albert of Belgium, and returned to Italy a few years later. Declared a charitable foundation in 1927, it was administered by joint commissions of the two countries, and the construction of houses for Italo-Belgian artists was planned. The tourist facilities of the area, including a popular inn, were only revived in the 1960s.

Balbianello

Built towards the end of the 18th century by Cardinal Angelo Maria Durini, who already owned the 16th-century Villa del Balbiano in Ossuccio, Villa del Balbianello stands on the Lavedo promontory, a magnificent panoramic site chosen by the Cardinal for its secluded position. The villa consists of two main buildings with a library, a music room, two drawing rooms and a large portico in a central position, designed so that both sides of the peninsula, facing towards Tremezzo and Isola Comacina, can be seen. Villa Balbianello has had some famous owners, such as the Porro Lambertenghi and Arconati Visconti families, who further embellished the structure; the last was Count Guido Monzino, a famous explorer who restored the original style of the furnishings and embellished the residence with valuable collec-

tions of Chinese, pre-Columbian and African art obtained on his expeditions. The sleigh he used to reach the North Pole in 1971 is exhibited in one of the rooms. The terraced garden exhibits particular care in the choice of plants, designed to create an attractive colour effect by mingling the blue of the lake with the vegetation. The villa, which was donated to FAI (the Italian Environment Fund) by Count Monzino in 1988, can be reached by boat from Sala Comacina. From the jetty visitors can walk to a small church standing on the site of a former Franciscan monastery; a tortuous route carefully designed to make the most of the view gradually introduces them to this wonderful corner of the lake.

Tremezzo

This town, which also boasts Roman origins (Curte Tremecia), was part of the defensive system of Isola Comacina in the Middle Ages. It was destroyed after Como retaliated against Milan's allies, but recovered and became part of the Visconti territory. A popular resort because of its particularly mild climate, it features some magnificent villas and exclusive hotels, mainly built between the 18th and 19th centuries, like the imposing Grand Hotel di Susino. In the hamlet of Bolvedro stands Villa La Quiete, with its magnificent Italianate garden, wrought iron gate and elegant furnishings. Built in the 18th century for Duke Del Carretto, it then passed to the Brentano family and the

Serbelloni family, whose tutor for many years was poet Giuseppe Parini. Next door is the 17th-century Villa La Carlia, which has a less imposing appearance but also has a magnificent garden. Particularly unusual is Villa Amila, built in the Rationalist style in the early 20th century for the Como branch of the Italian Motor Boat Association.

Churches worth visiting include S. Maria in the hamlet of Rogaro, which contains the statue of a Black Madonna dating from the late 17th century and a copy of the miraculous Madonna of Einsiedlen, and the church of S. Vincenzo at Portezza, with its lovely Romanesque belltower dating from 1100.

Villa Carlotta

Just beyond the Tremezzo lakeside walk stands Villa Carlotta, one of the most majestic villas in Italy, built towards the end of the 17th century on the orders of Marquis Giorgio II Clerici on a small hill that slopes gently down to the lake. Marquis Clerici, the heir to a huge fortune made in the silk trade, was also a senator and speaker of the Senate in 1717. His son and grandson died young, and he left his entire fortune to his great-grandson Antonio Giorgio, who completed the construction and layout of the building. First a soldier, then a diplomat to the court of Maria Teresa of Austria, he soon squandered the family assets, and his daughter Claudia inherited nothing but the villa at Tremezzo, which she sold to Gian Battista Sommaria in 1801. This shady character had accumulated a large fortune by dubious means which he invested in the purchase of numerous

works of art, perhaps to rehabilitate his image, and perhaps to compete with his political rival Francesco Melzi, who owned a villa at Bellagio. Sommaria decorated the rooms of the villa with exquisite works of art, such as Cupid and Psyche by Adamo Tavolini (a copy of the work of the same name by Canova), the Maddalena by Canova, a frieze portraying The Entry of Alexander the Great into Babylon by Thorwaldsen, busts by Fontana and Acquisti, and paintings by Hayez and Wicar. The rooms were sumptuously decorated to provide the right setting for the numerous receptions held there, whose celebrated guests included French authors Stendhal and Flaubert. On the death of the Marquis in 1826, his relatives sold much of the property. The villa, with its art collection, was sold in 1843 to Princess Marianne of Nassau, who gave it as a dowry to her

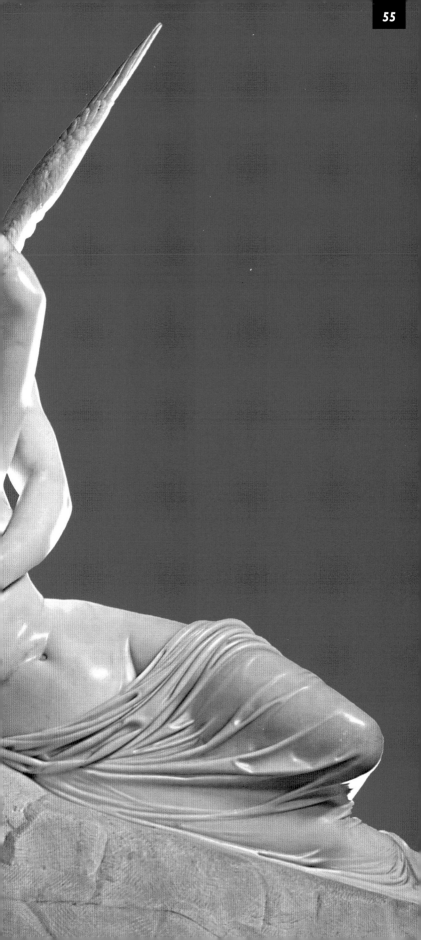

daughter Charlotte when she married Grand Duke George of Saxony-Meiningen. The dukes of Saxony-Meiningen, who kept the property until the First World War, mainly used the villa as a holiday home, and sold some valuable works of art, but extended the botanical garden and added some new exotic species. After various difficulties the Villa Carlotta charitable foundation was set up in 1927, and has worked to preserve and promote this valuable building ever since. The Foundation, working in liaison with the Environmental and Architectural Heritage

Department, recently reorganised the rooms in a way that recalls the particular neoclassical atmosphere of Sommariva's time. Today, Villa Carlotta is not only a magnificent residence that houses numerous works of art, but also has a wonderful garden which has evolved over the years according to the desires of the owners, and now, in a setting of fountains, balustrades and statues, contains some wonderful plants, including rhododendrons, azaleas, camellias, citrus fruit trees and a lovely bamboo grove inspired by Zen gardens.

Cadenabbia

This small town, which stands on the slopes of Mount Crocione, is named after the quiet landing stage (Ca' dei Nauli) once used by the boatmen who transported cargoes along the lake. The first tourist amenities were built in the early 19th century, and in later decades the village attracted famous guests like Stendhal, Giuseppe Verdi, Queen Victoria, and such a large English community that one of the first Anglican churches in Italy was needed. Among the most architectur-ally interesting villas are the ones built by Giacomo and Carlo Mantegazza in the late 19th and early 20th century: Villa Maria, Villa Guaita and Castello Ronconi. On the ruins of a Mediaeval tower stands Villa Collina, the headquarters of the Adenauer Foundation, set up in memory of the states-man, who lived there for over 20 years. Verdi composed La Traviata at Villa Margherita in the hamlet of Majolica, now owned by famous music pub-lishers Ricordi. A steep mule

track leads to the church of S. Martino, dating from the 16th century. The parish church of saints Naborre and Felice, built in the early 18th century, is situated in the town. Along the route leading from Lake Lugano to Crocetta di Menaggio stands the Griante castle, where Giovanni the Mad, a soldier and pirate who put the region to fire and sword, was executed in 1521, and some people still claim to see his ghost haunting the lake on stormy nights.

Menaggio

Situated at the start of the valley of the same name, where Via Regina forks west to Switzerland and north towards the upper Lario area, the town is divided into three hamlets: Croce and Loveno on the hillside, and Nobiallo by the lakeside. In view of its strategic position, Menaggio was probably the first point of contact for Celts coming from the north and Ligurians arriving from the south. The area was certainly inhabited in Roman times, as demonstrated by a tombstone dating from the 1st century A.D.. During the Longobard period the area was a major military stronghold, but it was not until the 10th century that a castle was built there, later extended by the addition of two towers. A particularly interesting tourist itinerary starts in the mediaeval part of the town, situated higher than the rest and featuring steep, narrow streets. The 19th-century part, with its large hotels and lido, is situated by the lake. At the end of Via Calvi stands the parish church of S. Stefano, probably built on the site of existing early Christian buildings, which has been altered several times. The interior is decorated with frescoes by Tagliaferri (1899) and various 17th- and 18th-century paintings; above the altar of the left-hand aisle hangs a copy of a painting by Bernardino Luini, the original of which was given to the French. The road up to the castle gives a good view of the elegant portals, and leads to a steep drop down to the Sanagra river. The castle, which dates from around the 10th century, was originally an impressive building, but was twice destroyed, the first time in 1124

by troops from Como, and the second in 1523 by Protestants from the nearby Grisons canton in Switzerland. The Baroque church of S. Carlo stands in the upper part of the town, on the ruins of the castle. The hamlet of Loveno contains the residential area of Menaggio. Of particular architectural and landscape interest is the 18th-century villa purchased by Enrico Mylius, a

rich businessman from Frankfurt, from the Carabelli family in 1829. Mylius extended the building, giving it a neoclassical style, and redesigned the park in the English style, adding numerous exotic plants. The interior contains an impressive collection of works of art, which the heirs of Mylius, the Vigoni family, have continued to expand. The villa currently houses an Italo-German culture centre.

Dongo

In the Middle Ages, Dongo, Sorico and Gravedona formed the county of Tre Pievi, one of the oldest counties in the lake area. The town was very important during that period, while in the 19th and 20th centuries the Albano plain was one of the first industrial centres, where the Falck steelworks was built. Nowadays the town is mainly a tourist destination, remembered mainly because it was here, on 28 April 1945, that the partisans stopped Mussolini and his Fascist officials who were fleeing to Switzerland. The Como Resistance Museum in Palazzo Manzi, a neoclassical building erected by Pietro Gilardoni in 1824, is dedicated to these events. The façade is rather austere, but the interior is sumptuous, especially the Gold Room, with its wealth of stuc-

coes and gilt, where aristocratic families once held magnificent balls and receptions. Another interesting building is the church of S. Stefano, of Romanesque origins but modified several times, which contains a 15th-century font and 16th-century frescoes. The 11th-century church of S. Maria di Martinico, also restored and modified, contains a valuable silver cross dating from 1513. An unusual place of worship is the sanctuary of the Madonna delle Lacrime (Madonna of Tears) or Madonna del Fiume (Madonna of the River), built to commemorate the miracle of a weeping Madonna in the early 17th century on the site of an ancient chapel which remained unharmed when the Albano river burst its banks.

Gravedona

This small town, which lies in the small gulf at the end of the Liro Valley, enjoys a particularly secluded position which makes it one of the favourite tourist spots in the area. Once inhabited by the Ligurians, the ancient houses perched along narrow streets and stairways betray its origins as a fishing village. At the time of Spanish rule the town was ceded to Cardinal Tolomeo Gallio, who in 1586 commissioned Pellegrino Tibaldi to build an imposing palazzo on the lakeshore. The building, with its square plan, has four keeps joined by porticoes, and a huge hall in the middle. After a chequered history, the palazzo is now owned by the West Upper Lario Mountain Community, and houses some valuable works of art. A magnificent example of Romanesque style is the church of S. Maria del Tiglio, built in the 12th century in the place where an early Christian baptistery once stood. The church is made of grey and white marble, and has an aisleless nave lined with loggias and arches and decorated with numerous 12th- and 13th-century frescoes, including an outstanding Last Judgement. Also worth a visit are the churches of S. Vincenzo (1050) and S. Maria delle Grazie, built in 1467 by Augustinian monks, where traces of the ancient frescoes can still be seen.

Domaso

Domaso, the historic rival of nearby Gravedona, is situated on the shore of the River Livo at the point where it flows into Lake Como. The mediaeval part of the town features steep, narrow streets that lead up from the lake towards the mountain, lined by walls which still bear traces of 15th-century frescoes. Since the 19th century the town has been extended along Via Regina, with numerous patrician villas. One of the most important buildings is the 18th-century Villa Camilla, which now houses the Town Hall, with its huge park and attractive frescoed rooms. Also worth a visit is the parish church of S. Bartolomeo, of Romanesque origins but later

renovated in Baroque style. The numerous paintings that decorate the interior include an altarpiece by Giulio Cesare Procaccino and an exquisite fresco dating from 1325, depicting a Madonna and Child, which was discovered in 1992. A paradise for lovers of nautical sports because of the constant breeze, called the Breva, that blows there, Domaso also offers some interesting dishes; in addition to the production of limited amounts of a wine that was apparently popular in Roman times, the ancient fishing tradition is kept alive with the famous missoltini (grilled dried fish).

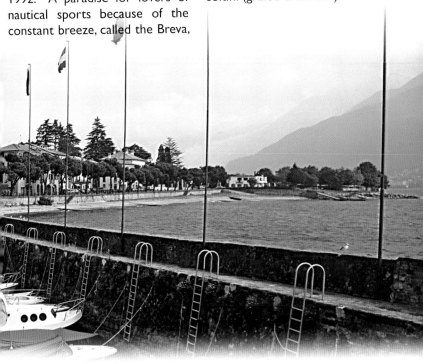

Bellagio

At their confluence, the two branches of Lake Como form a triangle, with its base between the small lakes of Alserio, Pusiano and Annone and its tip at the promontory which culminates in Mount San Primo. Right at the tip of this strip of land lies Bellagio, the "pearl of the Lario", which has been chosen as a residence since ancient times by authors, artists and poets, fascinated by the spectacular views and climate. The climate was so mild that olives could be grown in the area, as recalled by the name of Oliveto Lario (the Lario olive grove) on the steepest shore of the Lecco branch of the lake, where an excellent olive oil is still produced. Bellagio has been inhabited since prehistoric times, and in the Middle Ages it was a small town fortified by walls and a castle. All that survives of the fortifications is the belltower of the basilica of S. Giacomo,

which was originally the north tower. The two buildings, both of which date from the 12th century, were renovated in the 17th century. The church contains some Romanesque sculptures and a Deposition attributed to Perugino. The old town stands on either side of Via Garibaldi, with a maze of picturesque streets that slope down to the lake. The road that runs alongside the park of Villa Serbelloni leads to Punta Spartivento and the small harbour, from which there is an excellent view of both branches of the lake. The elegant 19th-century façades of the world-famous hotels give onto the lakeside promenade: the Grand Hotel Villa Serbelloni, at the foot of the villa built at the top of the promontory, the Hotel Du Lac, the Florence and the Excelsior. The end of the promontory is part of the estate once owned by the Serbelloni family, with its

huge walled park in which gardens alternate with woods. The building that became the main villa was a country house built in the 15th century on the ruins of a mediaeval castle, in the place where the villa of Pliny the Younger, called Tragoedia, probably stood. Bought by the son of Marquis Stanca in 1485 and converted into a villa, it was later owned by the Sfrondati family, who renovated it in 1533, and was inherited by the rich Serbelloni family in 1788. The large terraced park and many of the surviving furnishings and works of art date from that period. The villa was abandoned during the Risorgimento, later

converted into a hotel, and finally bought by the Rockefeller Foundation, which uses it as a prestigious venue for seminars and conferences. Equally famous is Villa Melzi, built in 1808-10 by architect Giocondo Albertolli for Francesco Melzi d'Eril, Vice-President of the Cisalpine Republic. The elegant neoclassical front overlooks the lake, and the villa is surrounded by an English-style garden full of statues and ponds. The villa is privately owned by the heirs and not open to the public, but it is possible to visit the pavilion, which has been turned into a museum, the garden and the chapel. There are

several other neoclassical villas near Bellagio: Villa Giulia, built by Count Pietro Venini in the late 18th century; Villa Trotti (1615), which belonged to the Loppio family and was rebuilt by Marquis Ludovico Trotti in the 19th century; and Villa Trivulzio, dating from the mid-18th century, which was once owned by the Poldi Pezzoli family, who extended it in the early years of the 19th century, the Trivulzio family and the Gerli family, who restored the Romanesque church of S. Maria that stands in the park. The 18th-century church of San Giovanni in the hamlet of the same name, which houses an altarpiece by Gaudenzio Ferrari portraying the Resurrection, is well worth a visit. From Bellagio, numerous boats and ferries carry passengers to other destinations on the left and right banks of Lake Como. A popular destination for walking or cycling trips is Piano del Tivano, crossed by Via Valassina which joins Bellagio to Erba. At the Ghisallo pass (754 m) stands a sanctuary, rebuilt in 1948 on 14th-century ruins, which is named after the Madonna of Ghisallo, patron saint of cyclists. Mount S. Primo, the highest mountain on the promontory (1685 m), is of no interest to climbers, but ideal for easy walks, and offers some magnificent views.

Nesso and Lezzeno

The largest inhabited area between Como and Bellagio is Nesso, a town divided into the hamlets of Castello, Vico and Careno. In mediaeval times it was a fortified town, with a castle that was destroyed by Francesco Sforza during the war against condottiero Giangiacomo Medici (known as Il Medeghino, 1531). All that survives is part of the walls and the towers. As well as the characteristic nucleus of stone houses built onto the mountainside, Nesso features some attractive churches (the mediaeval parish church of SS. Pietro and Paolo, the Romanesque church of S. Maria in the hamlet of Vico, and the 12th-century church of S. Martino at Careno) and spectacular scenery unique in the area, such as the Nesso gorge and the Masera grotto with its inner lake. The gorge, formed by the Tuf and Nosè rivers which flow through

the town, consists of a narrow ravine through which a waterfall crashes. A Romanesque bridge known as the "Civera" bridge joins the small towns of Coatesa and Riva di Castello. Climbing towards the northernmost tip of the Como Triangle we come to Lezzeno, a lakeside town of ancient Celtic and Ligurian origins. Its churches include the 16th-century parish church of SS. Quirico and Giulitta, the 15th-century oratory of the Madonna del Ceppo (in the hamlet of Pescaù), and the sanctuary of the Madonna delle Lacrime, built in 1690 to commemorate the miracle of a weeping statute of the Madonna. The Carpe grotto, also known as the Bulberi or Blue Grotto, offers an attractive spectacle of light and colour between the walls of the Sassi Grosgalli high above the lake.

Lecco

Lecco is built on the shore of "the branch of Lake Como that extends southwards", as described by Manzoni at the start of The Betrothed. Together with its traditional rival, Como, Lecco is the most important town on the lake, and is the capital of the Lecco province, which stretches along the valleys of the Lombardy pre-Alps. Situated at the point where the River Adda flows out of the lake, it is surrounded by some of the best-known peaks of these mountains: on one side the harsh silhouette of the Grigne and Resegone, and on the other the softer profile of the Corni di Canzo and Monte Barro. A town of ancient origins, once inhabited by the Goths and Longobards, Lecco was officially founded with that name in 845, as a district under Frankish rule. The first ring of walls enclosing the nucleus around the castle dates from that period. Lecco was important because of its strategic position, and was an active trading centre by 1100. It first came under the rule of the Archbishopric of Milan, was then fought over by the Della Torre family and the Viscontis, who razed the town to the ground in 1296, and was finally subjugated by the Milanese duchy in 1335. Azzone Visconti strengthened its defensive system by completing the city walls to form a triangle with the tip facing

north and the base on the lakeside, and built the fortified bridge over the River Adda (1336-38), still in use today, which is the symbol of the town. Defended at either end by a tower with a drawbridge, the bridge originally had eight spans, and three more were added later to aid the flow of the waters. The Ponte Vecchio (old bridge), which has been restructured several times, represents the historic memory of the town: it was fought over throughout the Middle Ages by mercenaries who attempted to take it first from the Visconti family, and later from the Sforza family, and was the site of a battle between the French and Austrian armies in 1779. As in the rest of the Como area, the years of Spanish rule brought economic stagnation, invasions, war, famine and plague. Lecco recovered under Austrian rule, with a series of political and administrative reforms and rebuilding of the town, to which it owes its present 19th-century appearance, for which architect Giuseppe Bovara was largely responsible. The oldest part of the town is situated between Piazza Cermenati, overlooking the lake, Piazza XX Settembre, and a maze of alleys that irradiate all around, still bearing the names of ancient guilds. This was the mediaeval quarter, where trade was concentrated and the market was

held until not long ago. The 15th-century Provost's House, whose inner courtyards, with porticoes and loggias, were restored during renovation work carried out in 1970-71, and Palazzo delle Paure, the ancient customs post at which taxes were paid, stand in the large Piazza Cermenati, named after the famous geologist from Lecco. Behind the piazza, in a raised position, stands the basilica of S. Nicolò, patron saint of sailors, renovated by Bovara in the neoclassical style. The basilica, built on the site of an existing Romanesque church, probably dating from the 13th century, had already been modified several times before this renovation, while the neogothic belltower, with its hexagonal plan, was added in 1882. The south façade retains traces of the original Romanesque church, and some valuable 14th-century frescoes have been found inside it, in the Baptistery chapel. The Visconti tower of the castle, which was demolished by the Austrians together with the city walls in

1782, can be glimpsed from Piazza XX Settembre, lined with porticoes. The tower was restored by Bovara in 1816, then turned into a prison, and now houses the Civic Museum of the Risorgimento and the Resistance. Another building by Bovara, Palazzo Bertarelli, with its elegant portico (1833-34), stands in the piazza. The most typically 19th-century part of Lecco is concentrated between Piazza Mazzini, Piazza Manzoni and Piazza Garibaldi, and includes Via Cavour, with its attractive neoclassical façades. From here we come to Piazza Diaz, with the Central Station and the Town Hall, housed in a building originally designed by Bovara as a hospital (1836) and converted around 1920. Piazza Garibaldi, where the 19th-century Teatro Sociale by Bovara stands, is surrounded by buildings constructed in the first half of the 20th century: the Law Courts (1938-41) and the headquarters of the Banca Popolare di Lecco (1941). Via Roma connects Piazza Garibaldi to the piazza

named after author Alessandro Manzoni, with his statue by sculptor Francesco Confalonieri (1891) standing in the middle. The sanctuary of Nostra Signora della Vittoria, dedicated to the soldiers who died in the First World War, contains numerous works of art saved from the destroyed convent of S. Giacomo, including a Crucifixion by Fra' Gerolamo Codega dating from the late 16th century. In the hamlet of Castello, one of the oldest settlements, stands the 18th-century Palazzo Belgioioso. Its U-shaped struc-

ture opens onto the garden, and the central part is ornamented by a row of porticoes and loggias. The Palazzo houses the Natural History Museum, with a room dedicated to Lecco geologist Antonio Stoppani, and the Archaeological Museum, which contains a collection of finds made in the province, ranging from prehistoric times to the late Middle Ages, and a metallurgy section. The most interesting stops on the Manzoni itinerary are concentrated between Caleotto and Pescarenico. The villa which belonged to the

Manzoni family from 1615 is situated in Caleotto. Rebuilt around 1770, it has two storeys built round a porticoed courtyard. The ground floor, whose furnishings date from 1818, the year when Manzoni sold the villa, houses the museum dedicated to Manzoni and the locations described in The Betrothed, while the first floor houses the Municipal Art Gallery. Pescarenico, not far from the Ponte Vecchio, still has the appearance of a fishing village in its houses with courtyards and wooden balconies overlooking the narrow streets. The parish church of SS. Lucia and Materno (1576) was once the church of Fra' Cristoforo's Capuchin monastery, but all that remains of the monastery is a courtyard and a few cells. Inside the church there is a 16th-century wooden altar, an altarpiece painted by Giovan Battista Crespi (1600), and some coloured wax sculptures of the Neapolitan school made towards the end of the 17th century.

Varenna

Varenna, with its enviable view of the three branches of the lake, stands on the slopes of a promontory at the mouth of the Esino river. Behind it soars the rocky silhouette of Mount San Defendente (1315 m), from which a valuable black and white marble was once quarried.

Although its origins are older, its history is linked to that of Isola Comacina: when the island was destroyed by Como in 1169 its inhabitants fled to Varenna, bringing with them wealth and traditions that still survive today. The famous Lake Festival, held on the first Saturday in July, commemorates the arrival of the survivors on what they called the Insula Nova. The ancient town overlooking the lake features steep, narrow streets with archways which fan out from the central piazza, and the ancient Roman forum, around which stand the parish church of S. Giorgio (1313), the Romanesque oratory of S. Giovanni Battista, and the 17th-century oratory of the Madonna delle Grazie. Since the mid-19th century Varenna has

found its vocation as a centre for international congresses, housed in Villa Monastero, Villa dei Cipressi and the Albergo Reale, once a manor house and spinning mill. The hamlet of Fiumelatte, near Varenna, has the shortest river in Italy (250 m). Mentioned by Leonardo in the Codice Atlantico because of its characteristic intermittent flow, it is also called "the river of the two Madonnas" because it appears around the feast of the Annunciation (25th March) and disappears around 7th October, the feast of the Madonna of the Rosary. The small town of Vezio, with its characteristic stone houses, is one of the oldest, as demonstrated by the numerous Iron Age relics found in the area. Here, on a rocky outcrop of Mount Fopp, stand the ruins of the fortress that once dominated Varenna, encircling the village with double walls that ran down to the lake. Vezio castle, reconstructed in the Middle Ages, is formed by a perimeter wall with a 20-metre tall square tower in the middle.

Colico

Colico, dominated by Mount Legnone, on the tip of the lake along the east bank, has always been an obligatory stage on the route to Val Chiavenna and the Alpine passes leading to Switzerland and Austria. Devastated over the centuries by the passage of foreign troops, plagues and periodic floods of the River Adda, it regained importance after 1858 with the creation of an artificial river bed and reclamation of the huge marshy area of Piano di Spagna, which has now been turned into a nature reserve where various bird species nest. The strategic importance of the area is demonstrated by the ruins of the Spanish fort of Fuentes, the last stronghold on the River Adda. In the hamlet of Olgiasca, where the lake forms an inlet called "laghetto di Piona", stands one of the most famous monuments on

the lake, the Cluniac Piona Abbey. The 11th-century church with its attractive wooden ceiling is decorated with frescoes of Byzantine inspiration, while the cloister, dating from 1257, is a rare example of the transition from the Romanesque to the Gothic style, with some beautiful capitals carved with floral motifs, every one of them different.

Piona Abbey

Typical Dishes

Missoltini with polenta

Risotto with perch fillets

Resta (Herringbone cake)